Vacation Time

WRITTEN BY ROBIN STANLEY

ILLUSTRATED BY RUSTY FLETCHER & TERRY JULIEN

ISBN 0-7847-1828-8

12 11 10 09 08 07 06   9 8 7 6 5 4 3 2 1

Standard
PUBLISHING
Bringing The Word to Life™

Cincinnati, Ohio

S0-BFA-637

The school year is over; vacation time is here! We'll have fun, but first we'll say, "Thank you, God, for rest and play."

God gives rest. —Psalm 127:2

Going to visit Grandma is a favorite summer treat.

She takes us to the zoo—

and helps us learn to skate. Thank you, God, for Grandma!

A nearby park is perfect for an all-day get-away.
We'll take a winding hike—

maybe watch some birds at play. It's good to stop and notice all the creatures God has made.

Stop and consider the wonderful miracles of God!
—Job 37:14

Even though we're not in school, every day's a day to learn. At the museum we discover dinosaurs that once had walked the earth.

And the men who made the first plane fly—

wanted to be like birds!

The excitement of the county fair gives our family great times to share!

Shout to God with joyful praise! —Psalm 47:1

No vacation is complete without some backyard fun. Camping out at night's the best! Pitch in, quick, before the sun is gone!

Some days we just need a break from all the stuff we do.
Mom brings us all together with a yummy barbeque!

Whether we're at rest or play, staying home, or out all day, we'll be sure to give God thanks for our fun vacation time!

It is good to give thanks to the LORD.
—*Psalm 92:1*